I Married a **Monster** from Outer Space!

Tear-and-Send Postcards from the Truly Terrible Fantasy and Science Fiction B-Films of the '40s and '50s

Selected by
Michael Barson

 Pantheon Books, New York

Introduction

You just never know when you might end up marrying a monster—the kind from Andromeda, that is—or a gorilla. Or when you might stumble upon a lost civilization of prehistoric Amazons, or find yourself turning into a wasp. It's always better to be prepared, and with that in mind we present you with this collection of posters featuring outré menaces from some of yesteryear's choicest fantasy, horror, and science fiction films. But be forewarned: *2001* these movies are not. And just as well.

If there's one thing these humble gems have in common, it's that they were usually made in eleven days on a budget of $75 by directors who were not named Welles, with actors who did not include Olivier or Brando (unless it was Tony Olivier and Chuck Brando). But then, the names Chaney, Montez, Graves, and Gabor are redolent of a more intoxicating fragrance for many of us than those others—and *our* underpaid, overworked, unappreciated thespians never compromised their dignity by chasing after Oscars and pretending that Eugene O'Neill is interesting. (It is to laugh!)

Most of these films are available on video today after years of being relegated to occasional appearances on The Late Show, and you might want to screen some to see just what kind of movie could be produced in two weeks. Then again, if you didn't, no one would blame you.

—Michael "Flash" Barson

SENSATIONAL!
SOFT ARMS KILLING WITH A VOODOO CURSE!
WEIRD WOMAN
AMAZING!
BRUTAL!
starring
LON CHANEY
ANNE GWYNNE EVELYN ANKERS
with
Lois Collier
Elisabeth Risdon
Ralph Morgan
Elizabeth Russell
A Realart RE-RELEASE

Weird Woman

(Universal, 1944) ✦ A tale of the occult based on Fritz Lieber's novel *Conjure Wife*, this was an installment in Universal's low-budget series of "Inner Sanctum" chillers. Lon Chaney, Jr. returns to his hometown with new bride Anne Gwynne, whom he plucked off a tropic isle, but old girlfriend Evelyn Ankers gets a mite jealous and begins cooking up some seriously bad voodoo. It was fun to see Chaney as a helpless normal guy after watching him play the Wolf Man, Frankenstein, Dracula, and the Mummy, and it was an equally nice switch to make career-victim Ankers the source of evil. The film was remade in 1962 as *Burn, Witch, Burn!* with a superior screenplay by horror veterans Charles Beaumont and Richard Matheson, but the poster wasn't nearly as much fun. This one dates from the 1952 re-release.

From *I Married a Monster from Outer Space* ✦ Compilation and New Text © 1994 Michael Barson ✦ Pantheon Books

HERE SOON!

Cobra Woman

MARIA MONTEZ and JON HALL with SABU

Directed by ROBERT SIODMAK

Produced by GEORGE WAGGNER

A UNIVERSAL PICTURE

GFD

Distributed by GENERAL FILM DISTRIBUTORS
127 Wardour St. W.1.

Cobra Woman

(Universal, 1944) ✦ Maria Montez was born Maria Africa Vidal de Santo Silas and became the cult star we now love with her roles in Technicolor extravaganzas like *Arabian Nights, White Savage,* and *Gypsy Wildcat.* But *Cobra Woman* was her crowning achievement, a tale of twin sisters on a tropical isle—one the demented high priestess Nadja, the other pure-hearted native girl Tollea. They both desire beefcake icon Jon Hall, but the dispute is resolved amicably when Good Maria helps Evil Maria trip on her high heels and fall through a castle window to her death. All this, and a chimp, the sacrificial Dance of the Cobra maidens, Sabu, and a rumbling volcano. It was directed by Robert Siodmak, who went on to even better things, while Montez continued as Hollywood's premier fantasy goddess (*Siren of Atlantis*) before suffering a fatal heart attack in her bathtub at the age of 31. In the 1955 *Cult of the Cobra,* Faith Domergue could actually change into a snake—a good career move.

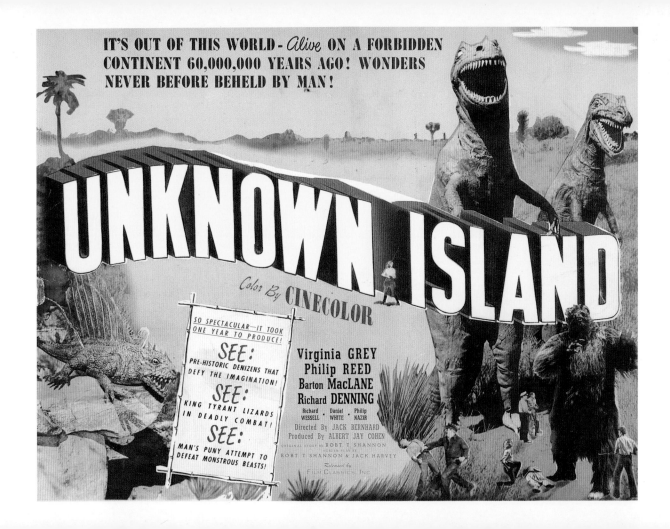

Unknown Island

(Film Classics, 1948) ✦ After the success of *King Kong* in 1933, everyone wanted to make their own dinosaur movie with awe-inspiring special effects. The trouble was, except for *Kong's* Willis O'Brien and his crack staff of stop-motion animators, no one knew how to do it. That left just two options: photograph real lizards and magnify them to look like giants, as Hal Roach did in 1940 for *One Million B.C.*, or dress up a few guys in rubber T-Rex suits and let them shamble around in the woods while the actors gasped in horror. Hello, *Unknown Island*, the first (but not the last!) film to implement this breakthrough in technical wizardry. What you got for your ticket was two saggy, baggy Ceratosaurs, one rubber Dimetrodon (lower left), and a blood-thirsty "giant sloth" (bottom right) that clearly was some schmuck in a moth-eaten ape suit—all blurrily rear-projected in the garish Cinecolor process. "One Year to Produce!" was its proud boast, but this looks more like six days in Aunt Rose's backyard.

From *I Married a Monster from Outer Space* ✦ Compilation and New Text © 1994 Michael Barson ✦ Pantheon Books

The WEIRDEST visitor the Earth has ever seen!

THE MAN FROM PLANET X

Sherrill Corwin presents

"The MAN from PLANET X"

starring ROBERT CLARKE · MARGARET FIELD · WILLIAM SCHALLERT

Directed by Edgar G. Ulmer · Written and Produced by Aubrey Wisberg and Jack Pollexfen · Released thru United Artists

The Man from Planet X

(United Artists, 1951) ✦ Moody, atmospheric, and unpredictable, *The Man from Planet X*—low-budget notwithstanding—compares favorably with the best of the science fiction films of the '50s. Brilliantly mounted by cult director Edgar (*Detour*) Ulmer, the film is set on a tiny island off the coast of Scotland. Affiliated Press reporter Robert Clarke is summoned to interview the astronomers tracking the flight of the mysterious Planet X, which shortly will intersect with the Earth's orbit most closely at this very isle. But one night lovely Margaret Field (mother of Sally) stumbles into an advance scout from Planet X while walking the moors, and he follows her back to her father's lab. Evil scientist William Schallert (Patty Duke's dad on TV fifteen years later) manhandles "the boogie," who responds by hypnotizing the entire village in preparation for the main invasion force (seems the poor blighters are dying out and need a new planet on which to start over). Moments before the alien is going to signal his compatriots that it's time to launch the invasion, Scotland Yard blows him and his spaceship to kingdom come. So much for First Contact.

From *I Married a Monster from Outer Space* ✦ Compilation and New Text © 1994 Michael Barson ✦ Pantheon Books

Bride of the Gorilla

(Jack Broder Productions, 1951) ✦ Curt Siodmak, younger brother of Oscar-nominated Robert Siodmak, wrote the screenplays for some of the forties' best horror movies, like *The Wolfman* and *I Walked With a Zombie*. But here he becomes a genuine auteur, both writing and directing this parable about the high cost of adultery. Raymond Burr—still svelte and pre-law—is a plantation manager who lusts after his boss's wife, voluptuous Barbara Payton. Burr kills the plantation owner with the help of a viper. But an old native hag who has witnessed the murder poisons Burr with a potion made from an illegal plant, and soon he begins to turn into a demon gorilla—or so he thinks; we see it only when he looks in a mirror, a nice touch. He spends every night running around the jungle tearing animals to shreds, returning in the morning caked with dried blood. Of course he meets his doom in the end, as cop Lon Chaney, Jr. muses about how the jungle always takes its revenge. Not as lurid (darn it!) as the poster suggests.

From *I Married a Monster from Outer Space* ✦ Compilation and New Text © 1994 Michael Barson ✦ Pantheon Books

The Most Fantastic Expedition Ever Conceived by Man!
FLIGHT TO MARS
starring
MARGUERITE CHAPMAN · CAMERON MITCHELL
with
ARTHUR FRANZ · VIRGINIA HUSTON · JOHN LITEL · MORRIS ANKRUM
Produced by
WALTER MIRISCH
Directed by
Lesley Selander
SCREENPLAY BY
ARTHUR STRAWN
COLOR BY
Cinecolor

Flight to Mars

(Monogram, 1951) ✦ The first science fiction film in color has a formulaic plot that nearly sinks it, but the well-executed art design and the stunning Marguerite Chapman make *Flight to Mars* worth viewing—though it can never be mentioned in the same breath as such 1951 classmates as *The Thing* and *The Day the Earth Stood Still.* An expedition crash-lands on Mars, and the earthlings are surprised to find the awaiting denizens to be not only friendly, but also dressed in used togs from *Destination Moon.* But the Martians have a hidden agenda: Desperately in need of uranium to survive, they plan to help the visitors repair their spaceship, then commandeer it and attack the Earth. Good Martian Marguerite Chapman—the leggiest scientist in the universe—tips off expedition leader Arthur Franz, with whom she's fallen in love. The earthlings escape at the last second, with their rocket leaving a trail of smoke that looks suspiciously like it came from a cigarette. Top-billed Cameron Mitchell has little to do as the writer assigned to the expedition except to give lonely hearts advice to Virginia Huston. Reportedly, *Flight to Mars* was shot in eleven days; I believe it.

From *I Married a Monster from Outer Space* ✦ Compilation and New Text © 1994 Michael Barson ✦ Pantheon Books

"UNTAMED WOMEN"

SAVAGE BEAUTIES WHO FEARED NO ANIMAL...YET FELL BEFORE THE TOUCH OF MEN!

A Jewell Enterprises Production   Released thru United Artists

Untamed Women

(United Artists, 1952) ✦ "Uncivilized cult rites! Prehistoric monsters! Barbaric women raiders...In an unbelievable world!" Air Force Captain Mikel Conrad and three of his crew members are washed ashore on an unknown island after their plane goes down at sea. Here things are run by Sandra, the High Priestess (Doris Merrick), whose tribe of fur-clad females is descended from the Druids. Sandra tries to ditch the guys in a valley loaded with dinosaurs, but fortunately for her the plan fails, as Conrad and his lads return just in time to save the Cro-Magnon cuties from a hostile tribe of murderous Neanderthal brutes. Their pitched battle is interrupted by the erupting volcano (stock footage from the 1940 opus *One Million B.C.*) and everyone dies except for Conrad, who escapes to tell the tale—which naturally gets him immediately committed. The film's producers suggested that theatre owners promote *Untamed Women* by putting two or three beautiful girls dressed in leopard-skin sarongs in a bamboo cage in the lobby. (How many complied has never been determined.) A worthy addition to the pantheon of Lost Worlds Ruled by Bimbos genre.

WEIRD! STARTLING! UNBELIEVABLE!

SEE! A 8 FT. SPIDER!

SEX SUPER WOMEN!

ON THE MESA OF

LOST WOMEN

J. FRANCIS WHITE and JOY N. HOUCK present

LOST WOMEN

STARRING

JACKIE COOGAN · RICHARD TRAVIS
ALLAN NIXON · LYLE TALBOT

CO-STARRING MARY HILL and ROBERT KNAPP

INTRODUCING TANDRA QUINN (THE TARANTULA GIRL)

WITH

CHRIS PIN MARTIN and SAMUEL WU

Directed by HERBERT TEVOS and RON ORMOND

Produced by MELVIN GORDON and WILLIAM PERKINS

A HOWCO PRODUCTION

On the Mesa of Lost Women

(Howco, 1953) ✦ Few of the films discussed in this collection qualify as "good" movies, although most of them provide some loopy fun. *On the Mesa of Lost Women*, however, is so inept that it takes a highly trained fan of the abysmal to make it through all 70-odd (*very* odd) minutes. Erstwhile child-star Jackie Coogan plays scientist Dr. Araña (Spanish for spider), whose mad plan for taking over the world involves turning spiders into beautiful women—in particular Tandra Quinn, "the tarantula girl"—or maybe it's vice versa. Anyway, his army of dwarves (don't ask) is routed by the first group of normal people lured atop the mesa, and the dream race of superwomen—a dream many of us share—is extinguished by an explosion. Or is it? The maddening "score" consists of a Mexican guitar strumming incessantly, totally divorced from the action onscreen. Wait—did I say "action"? Never mind.

From *I Married a Monster from Outer Space* ✦ Compilation and New Text © 1994 Michael Barson ✦ Pantheon Books

"THE NEANDERTHAL MAN"

He held them all in the grip of deadly terror ...nothing could keep him from this woman he claimed as his own!

HALF MAN ...HALF BEAST...

STARRING
ROBERT SHAYNE
RICHARD CRANE
DORIS MERRICK
JOYCE TERRY
Directed by E. A. DUPONT
Written and Produced by
AUBREY WISBERG and
JACK POLLEXFEN
A WISBERG-POLLEXFEN PRODUCTION
PRESENTED BY GLOBAL PRODUCTIONS
RELEASED THRU UNITED ARTISTS

The Neanderthal Man

(United Artists, 1953) ✦ A scientist (Robert Shayne) regresses his evolutionary development 400,000 years by injecting himself with a serum that reactivates dormant memory cells. The next thing you know, he and his house cat, who's been regressed into a full-size sabre-toothed tiger, are terrorizing the local deer and cattle. Soon, of course, they've worked their way up to human prey. Shayne kidnaps his fiancée (Doris Merrick of *Untamed Women*), but before he can decide what to do with her, his 750-pound tabby attacks him and they fight to the death. You may be saying to yourself, "What an unlikely tale!"—but as the film's promotional materials assure us, "Due to the care and research that the producers put into the film, the thrilling story never enters the realm of implausibility." (Well, that settles *that*.) Newspapermen Aubrey Wisberg and Jack Pollexfen, who wrote and produced *The Neanderthal Man*, also performed those duties for *Problem Girls* as well as for the fine *The Man from Planet X*. The great Beverly Garland, who's pictured all over the poster, appears only briefly as one of the Neanderthal Man's victims. The de-evolution process was dramatized again in the 1958 film *Monster on the Campus* and in 1980's *Altered States*, among others.

Cat-Women of the Moon

(Astor, 1953) ✦ "There *can't* be another world in the bowels of the moon!" Oh, yes, there can! And I bet it's populated by black-leotarded dames with telepathic powers and names like "Lambda." That's who Sonny Tufts and his expedition from Earth find waiting for them when they land on the moon. Feigning friendliness, the cat-women really want to steal the earthlings' spaceship and travel to our humble world, where they can mate with the despised inhabitants in order to repopulate their decimated race. ("We will choose your men eugenically...the best of the Earth mongrels will be none too good!") First they must seduce the schlubby Commander Laird, who as embodied by Tufts should have been renamed "Lard" (he appears to have been snacking on Twinkies, washed down with scotch, all the way across the galaxy). To that end they regale the expedition members with a ritual dance, then hypnotize Marie Windsor, the only earthwoman along for the ride, to help them con the earthmen out of their secrets and spacesuits (although the one named Walt complains to one cat-woman, "You're too smart for me, baby—I like 'em stupid!"). But just in the nick of time, Tufts and his men get wise and blast the cat-women (off-camera) before they can steal Moon Rocket #4. Originally released in 3-D.

Devil Girl From Mars

(Spartan, 1954) ✦ This low-budget British production didn't receive a wide release in the United States, but its cast of no-names—Patricia Laffan, Hugh McDermott, and Hazel Court—and nigh-actionless story probably wouldn't have created a stampede to the box office in any event. Devil Girl Nyah (Laffan) gets lost on her way to London and lands her flying saucer in the Scottish highlands near the Bonnie Charlie Inn, where she's in search of lusty, able-bodied men to bring back to Mars (which is apparently suffering a shortage to rival today's New York City). Assisted by her clanking robot appliance Chani, she atomizes a few trees and a villager to prove she means business. But in that skintight, black-leather outfit, she should have had them lining up in droves to follow her into space! Instead, the silly Scots blow up her flying saucer with her in it, spoiling the possibilities of a sequel about this intergalactic dominatrix.

PLACE
FIRST
CLASS
STAMP
HERE

THE LAST WORD IN SCIENCE-FICTION THRILLS!

KILLERS FROM SPACE

See the space killers plan to wipe out the human race!
See strange monsters, flying saucers, giant creatures . . .
SENSATIONAL!

with
PETER GRAVES
BARBARA BESTAR

Distributed by
R K O RADIO
PICTURES

A

Produced and Directed by W. LEE WILDER · Screenplay by BILL RAYNOR · From a story by MYLES WILDER

Killers from Space

(RKO, 1954) ✦ Nuclear scientist Peter Graves appears to be deceased, but he is brought back to life by the goofiest trio of aliens ever to grace the silver screen. The scene where Graves awakens and scopes out the threesome with their ping-pong-ball eyes and state of the art sweatshirts remains his finest piece of acting. These fearsome "killers" intend to conquer the earth with the most run-down bunch of electronic junk since *Sanford & Son*, but the resourceful Graves blows up their "VU" meters and saves the planet from laughing itself to death. Graves had been in *Red Planet Mars* in 1952, which remains the only time God and the Commies ever teamed up in a science fiction film. The eye-popping special effects were orchestrated by Harry Thomas, who also labored on *Superman and the Mole Men* and *The Neanderthal Man*, and who has recently gone on record stating that the producers of these films made him cut corners to such a degree that "sometimes the quality was lost." Hard to believe. Director W. Lee Wilder, whose previous science fiction entry was *Phantom from Space*, was the great Billy Wilder's brother, but *Double Indemnity* this isn't.

From *I Married a Monster from Outer Space* ✦ Compilation and New Text © 1994 Michael Barson ✦ Pantheon Books

Target Earth

(Allied Artists, 1954) ✦ "Paralyzed with fear?" Paralyzed with boredom is more like it. Richard Denning, fresh from his demise as the nasty scientist in *The Creature from the Black Lagoon*, wakes up one morning to find himself virtually alone in Chicago after an invasion of robots (from Venus? Mebbe) has caused a mass evacuation. The film's opening scenes, with Denning scuffling around trying to orient himself, searching for other refugees and provisions, are strong. But once Denning and the fetching Kathleen Crowley run into a pair of bickering tipplers and an escaped convict, *Target Earth* turns into a summer-stock revival of *The Petrified Forest*. Denning's trademark crankiness wears thin after a few minutes, and most of the "action" takes place in hotel rooms. The aliens themselves are a joke—pincered robots cobbled together from cardboard boxes, garden hose, and pie plates. They're finally defeated when scientist Whit Bissel, another alumnus from *Black Lagoon*, devises a subsonic frequency that cracks their transistors. But it's just such a snore as this that most needs a great poster to lure in the masses, and that *Target Earth* decidedly has.

From *I Married a Monster from Outer Space* ✦ Compilation and New Text © 1994 Michael Barson ✦ Pantheon Books

Revenge of the Creature

(Universal, 1955) ✦ Few sequels measure up to the original film, but *Revenge of the Creature* comes reasonably close to *Creature from the Black Lagoon*. It helped that both were helmed by Jack Arnold, the decade's preeminent director of thrill-packed SF (*The Incredible Shrinking Man, Tarantula, It Came From Outer Space*), and that Ricou Browning again donned the monster's scaly suit for the underwater sequences. But the Florida setting, where the captured Creature has been transported by John Agar, is not as evocative as the faux South America of the first film, and Lori Nelson—in the key role as the object of desire—is not on par with the sublime Julie Adams. The Creature's rampage is more understandable in the sequel, as Agar and sidekick John Bromfield have cruelly tortured him with electric cattle prods while "studying" him in his Marineland tank. Both pics were filmed in 3-D, although few moviegoers saw them projected in that format. The third film in the cycle, *The Creature Walks Among Us* (1956), further poured on the pathos as the Creature is operated upon to become half-human.

From *I Married a Monster from Outer Space* ✦ Compilation and New Text © 1994 Michael Barson ✦ Pantheon Books

It Conquered the World

(AIP, 1956) ✦ This is what happens when you design your poster art before making the film, the standard methodology of American International Pictures. Produced and directed by six-day wonder Roger Corman, *It Conquered the World* offers one of the big screen's more ridiculous monsters: a Venusian conehead who's *all* head (and mouth), with little arms stuck on where its ears should be. (This pile of papier-mâché, designed and worn by makeup-man Paul Blaisdell, showed what one could do on a budget of $14.95.) As the first earthman enslaved by the monster, Lee Van Cleef shows his flair for the dastardly. But when the creature kills his wife, Van Cleef comes to his senses and strikes back, toasting the overgrown turnip with a blowtorch, in a battle royal that costs him his own life as well. As usual, hero Peter Graves survives the fracas, although he does have to eliminate his own wife after he learns that she's under the creature's control. (Call it irreconcilable differences.) Corman and co-screenwriter (with Lou Rusoff) Charles Griffith would combine their talents the following year on the formidable double bill, *Attack of the Crab Monsters* and *Not of This Earth*, while Garland next appeared in Corman's *Swamp Women*.

From *I Married a Monster from Outer Space* ✦ Compilation and New Text © 1994 Michael Barson ✦ Pantheon Books

THE SCREAM THAT SHOCKS THE SCREEN WITH 300,000 VOLTS OF Horror!

Indestructible MAN

INHUMAN! INVINCIBLE! INESCAPABLE!

starring LON CHANEY

with MARIAN CARR

Casey Adams • Ross Elliot

SCREENPLAY BY VY RUSSELL and SUE BRADFORD

PRODUCED AND DIRECTED BY JACK POLLEXFEN

An ALLIED ARTISTS Picture

The Indestructible Man

(Allied Artists, 1956) ✦ A throwback to the days when the crime and horror genres merged together—
The Walking Dead (1936), *The Man They Could Not Hang*, *Man-Made Monster*, and *The Monster and the Girl*
(1941) come to mind—*The Indestructible Man* sent a wrongfully executed man on a pitiless mission of revenge
against those who betrayed him. Although this low-budget thriller was made in 1956, it resembled those earlier
horror movies and not the science fiction films of its own era. Known as The Butcher, and brought back from the
dead by a scientist, the now indestructible but mute (no lines to memorize!) Chaney reprises the kind of sham-
bling destruction he made famous in the old days (when he wasn't donning the guise of The Wolf Man and
Count Alucard). After getting toasted by flamethrowers while hiding in the sewers of L.A., he finally eradicates
himself by eating a million or so volts at a power station. Chaney would soon return for more abuse in *The
Alligator People*.

From *I Married a Monster from Outer Space* ✦ Compilation and New Text © 1994 Michael Barson ✦ Pantheon Books

PLACE
FIRST
CLASS
STAMP
HERE

From Hell It Came

(Allied Artists, 1957) ✦ For those denizens of the fifties tired of attacks by giant insects, aliens from Mars, revivified dinosaurs, and amoeba-like blobs, *From Hell It Came*, with its ludicrous walking, scowling tree stump, was the monster pic with a difference. Set on the well-known island of Kalai, the film begins with the execution of a native named Prince Kimo, who's interred in a wooden coffin with a knife buried to the hilt in his chest. But Kimo swears to return to take vengeance, and—by gosh!—he does. A stump begins to grow from his grave, and a group of American scientists who have come to the island to treat the natives for radiation burns digs it up and takes it into their laboratory for study. Oddly enough, the stump has developed a permanent scowl, and also seems to have a knife handle sticking out of it. You don't think...? Yes, it's the dreaded Tabanga!, the walking Tree of Revenge, which the spirit of Kimo has inhabited (or vice versa). Looking like nothing so much as the angry apple trees that pelted Dorothy with their fruit in *The Wizard of Oz*, the Tabanga was designed by the ubiquitous Paul Blaisdell.

From *I Married a Monster from Outer Space* ✦ Compilation and New Text © 1994 Michael Barson ✦ Pantheon Books

FEMALE MONSTER!

THEY CREATED AN INHUMAN BEING WHO DESTROYED EVERYTHING SHE TOUCHED!

SHE DEVIL

The woman they couldn't kill!

starring **MARI** · **JACK** · **ALBERT**
BLANCHARD · KELLY · DEKKER

Featuring JOHN ARCHER · FAY BAKER · BLOSSOM ROCK · PAUL CAVANAGH · Story "The Adaptive Ultimate" by JOHN JESSEL

Produced and Directed by **KURT NEUMANN** · Screenplay by **CARROLL YOUNG** and **KURT NEUMANN**

A REGAL FILMS, INC. PRODUCTION · Released by 20th CENTURY-FOX

A **REGALSCOPE** PICTURE

She Devil

(20th Century-Fox, 1957) ✦ When doctors Jack Kelly and Albert Dekker look for a guinea pig on whom to try their experimental fruit-fly extract, they come up with willing volunteer Mari Blanchard, who is dying of tuberculosis. (Well, these were the days before HMOs.) The serum works but has unfortunate side effects, like turning bombshell Mari into a conniving, remorseless thief and killer, and (even worse) changing her hair from brunette to blonde. When the doctors realize what a monster they've created, they inject her again with an antidote and let her die of TB; so much for "the woman they couldn't kill!" *She Devil* was based on the 1930s pulp story "The Adaptive Ultimate" by SF great Stanley G. Weinbaum. Director Kurt Neumann had more luck with the following year's *The Fly*, in which an insect and a human once again cross paths—literally.

NEW THRILLS! NEW SHOCKS!
NEW TERROR!
"Beginning OF THE END"
FILMED IN NEW HORRORSCOPE!
starring
PETER GRAVES · PEGGIE CASTLE · MORRIS ANKRUM
with THOMAS B. HENRY · THAN WYENN · JAMES SEAY
Produced and Directed by BERT I. GORDON · Screen Play by Fred Freiberger and Lester Gorn · An AB-PT Picture · Distributed by REPUBLIC PICTURES CORPORATION

Beginning of the End

(Republic Pictures, 1957) ✦ When a horde of giant grasshoppers appears in the Illinois countryside and begins consuming the citizenry for brunch, government research biologist Peter Graves has a nagging hunch that his radioactive growth accelerant might have contributed to the phenomenon. Sure enough, it turns out that the critters snuck into his greenhouse and helped themselves to his special vitamins. Now they're the size of elephants. The assembled might of the U.S. Army can't dissuade the rampaging beasties from crawling over Chicago's skyscrapers and rudely snacking on unwary tenants, but Graves has a plan. Aided by intrepid news-magazine photographer Peggie Castle, fresh from Roger Corman's *Oklahoma Woman*, Graves develops a signal that mimics the insects' mating whine, and broadcasts it so the grasshoppers follow it right into the ocean, saving mankind for at least another twenty minutes. Producer/director Bert I. Gordon (*The Amazing Colossal Man*) stole what he could from 1954's vastly superior *Them!*, then had the nerve to boast that at least his giant bugs were real. (So was Lassie.) 1957 was the big year for big bug attacks, with *The Monster That Challenged the World* (a caterpillar), *The Deadly Mantis*, *Monster from Green Hell* (wasps), and *The Black Scorpion*.

From *I Married a Monster from Outer Space* ✦ Compilation and New Text © 1994 Michael Barson ✦ Pantheon Books

I Married a Monster from Outer Space!

(Paramount, 1958) ✦ Sounds a lot sillier than it plays. Gloria Talbott, having recovered from the strain of appearing in both halves of Bert Gordon's 1957 double-bill, *Cyclops* and *Daughter of Dr. Jekyll*, essays the plum role of a bride who learns on her wedding night that there's something *different* about her husband. (No, not *that*.) Seems he's been possessed by an alien "from the Andromeda constellation" who's bent on relocating permanently in Tom Tryon's body. Naturally, no one believes her, even though other duplications begin to take place around town. Gloria's paranoia is effectively counterpointed by Tryon's growing fascination with his Earth body and its unpredictable emotions. As the Andromedans, whose own women have died off, muse on their mission while sitting in a bar one night pretending to drink (they can't abide alcohol), "Our scientists are working on a way right now to mutate human female chromosomes so we can have children with them. Believe it or not, it *can* be fun." (That's the spirit, boys!) Despite the low budget, the film compares favorably with Don Siegel's 1956 classic, *Invasion of the Body Snatchers*, improvising on the concept without simply ripping it off.

From *I Married a Monster from Outer Space* ✦ Compilation and New Text © 1994 Michael Barson ✦ Pantheon Books

MANKIND'S FIRST FANTASTIC FLIGHT TO **VENUS**—The Female Planet!

QUEEN OF OUTER SPACE

COLOR BY DE LUXE CinemaScope

An ALLIED ARTISTS Picture starring **ZSA ZSA GABOR**

ERIC FLEMING
LAURIE MITCHELL
LISA DAVIS

From a Story by BEN HECHT • Produced by BEN SCHWALB • Directed by EDWARD BERNDS • Screenplay by CHARLES BEAUMONT

Queen of Outer Space

(Allied Artists, 1958) ✦ They don't make 'em any funnier than this. Start with the inimitable Zsa Zsa Gabor as a Venusian scientist who works in her lab wearing a skintight evening dress; add Laurie Mitchell as the disfigured Venusian queen who hates all men because of radiation burns she suffered during "their" wars; throw in an expedition of wisecracking hepcats from Earth; season with a giant rubber spider/crab and a "Beta-Disintegrator" obviously constructed of cardboard and Alcoa-Wrap—and you might just begin to comprehend the looniness of this interplanetary Iliad. The story was credited to the great Ben Hecht, but surely he didn't contribute such dialogue as: "26,000,000 miles from Earth—and the little dolls are just the same!" . . . "How can a doll as cute as that be such a pain in the neck?" . . . and, "There's a certain irony in the fact that our lives, and perhaps the lives of everyone on Earth, may depend on Captain Patterson's sex appeal." (But then, director Ed Bernds *did* have a number of Three Stooges flicks on his resume.) Eric Fleming wears the same space duds the expedition sported in *Forbidden Planet* in 1956. After this, Fleming's next gig—herding cattle on television's *Rawhide*—must have felt like performing in *Hamlet*.

From *I Married a Monster from Outer Space* ✦ Compilation and New Text © 1994 Michael Barson ✦ Pantheon Books

A BEAUTIFUL WOMAN BY DAY– A LUSTING QUEEN WASP BY NIGHT.
The WASP WOMAN
STARRING
SUSAN CABOT · FRED EISLEY
BARBOURA MORRIS
Produced and Directed by ROGER CORMAN
Written by LEO GORDON

The Wasp Woman

(Allied Artists, 1959) ✦ Susan Cabot plays the head of a cosmetics firm who's panicking over the crow's feet that are becoming more noticeable with each visit to the mirror. Enter Michael Marks as a chemist who's discovered that wasp enzymes can reverse the aging process. Susan shoots up, and the years peel away like onionskin. But there's a hideous side effect: the injections transform Cabot into a werewasp at night, in which form she kills with abandon and drinks her victim's blood. Her reign of (extremely unconvincing) terror ends when hero Fred Eisley shoves her out a window. In death, the monster devolves into a bunch of buzzing wasps—except the bugs are really *bees*. So much for F/X. (Well, at least the *poster* is a shocker.) One of the lamest of Corman's fifties' flicks, from the office-bound mise-en-scène to the cardboard performances by the supporting cast to the wretched score by Fred Katz. Directing? Don't ask. (Where did Corman *get* his rep, anyway?) Cabot, who also starred in such Corman productions as *Sorority Girl* and *The Viking Women and the Sea Serpent*, was beaten to death in 1986 by her son.

From *I Married a Monster from Outer Space* ✦ Compilation and New Text © 1994 Michael Barson ✦ Pantheon Books

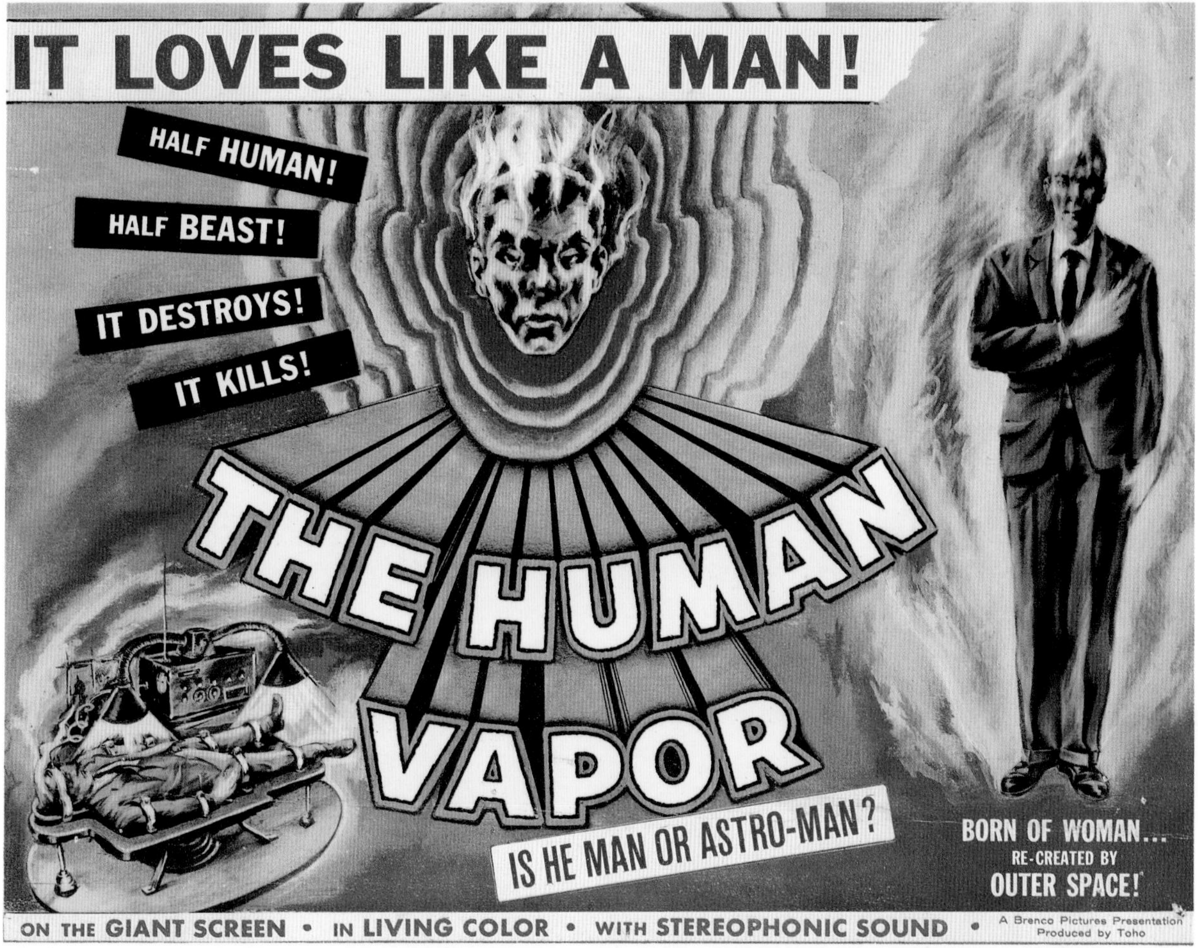
IT LOVES LIKE A MAN!
HALF HUMAN!
HALF BEAST!
IT DESTROYS!
IT KILLS!
THE HUMAN VAPOR
IS HE MAN OR ASTRO-MAN?
BORN OF WOMAN...
RE-CREATED BY
OUTER SPACE!
ON THE GIANT SCREEN • IN LIVING COLOR • WITH STEREOPHONIC SOUND •
A Brenco Pictures Presentation
Produced by Toho

The Human Vapor

(Toho, 1960) ✦ You've got to hand it to the Japanese movie industry; when they run out of giant radioactive dinosaurs (*Godzilla*), giant insects (*Mothra*), and giant prehistoric birds from outer space (*Rodan!*), they simply turn to regular-sized humans who have been turned into ravenous green slime by exposure to a hydrogen bomb (*The H Man*). In *The Human Vapor* we have a man who can turn himself into mist thanks to power siphoned from the stars. But when The Vapor uses that power to rob banks by wafting through keyholes to steal money for squandering on a dancer named Fujichiyo—well, that's an abuse of science that we simply cannot tolerate. This variation on *The Invisible Man* was pretty silly, and eager moviegoers were no doubt disappointed to find that "It Loves Like a Man!" referred only to The Human Vapor buying some roses for his girlfriend, and not shots of him practicing some alien erotic techniques. But hey, that's what posters are for.

From *I Married a Monster from Outer Space* ✦ Compilation and New Text © 1994 Michael Barson ✦ Pantheon Books